D1366030

Home

Jean Harrison

CHILDREN'S RIGHTS

Home

Jean Harrison

A+
Smart Apple Media

First published in 2004 by Evans Brothers Limited in association with Save the Children UK.
2A Portman Mansions
Chiltern Street
London, W1U 6NR

This edition published under license from Evans Brothers Limited. All rights reserved.

Copyright © 2004 Evans Brothers Limited and the Save the Children Fund.

Published in the United States by Smart Apple Media
2140 Howard Drive West, North Mankato, Minnesota 56003

U.S. publication copyright © 2005 Smart Apple Media
International copyright reserved in all countries.
No part of this book may be reproduced in any form without written permission from the publisher.
Printed in China

Library of Congress Cataloging-in-Publication Data

Harrison, Jean.
Home / by Jean Harrison.
p. cm. — (Children's rights)
Includes index.
ISBN 1-58340-418-X
1. Homelessness—Juvenile literature. 2. Right to housing—Juvenile literature. 3. Children's rights—Juvenile literature. I. Title. II. Series.

HV4493.H375 2004
363.5'93—dc22   2004041702

9 8 7 6 5 4 3 2 1

Credits:

Series editor: Louise John
Editor: Nicola Edwards
Designer: Simon Borrough
Producton: Jenny Mulvanny

Acknowledgements

Cover: Jenny Matthews
Title page: Jenny Matthews
p6: Howard Davies
p7: Michael Amendolia/Network
p8a: Jenny Matthews
p8b: Jon Spaull
p9: Neil Cooper and Jan Hammond
p10: Michael Amendolia/Network
p11a: Michael Amendolia/Network
p11b: Michael Amendolia/Network
p12: Jenny Matthews
p13: Howard Davies
p14a: John Pierre Joyce
p14b: James Brabazon
p15: Howard Davies
p16: James Brabazon/SCUK
p17: Dan White
p18: Tim Hetherington/Network/SCUK
p19a: Tim Hetherington/Network/SCUK
p19b: Tim Hetherington/Network/SCUK
p20: Tim Hetherington/Network
p21: Dan White
p22: Tim Hetherington/Network
p23: Tim Hetherington/Network
p24a: Tim Hetherington/Network
p24b: Dario Mitidieri
p25: Michael Amendolia/Network
p26: Stuart Freedman/Network Photographers/SCUK
p27a: Stuart Freedman/Network Photographers/SCUK
p27b: Stuart Freedman/Network Photographers/SCUK

Contents

All children have rights

The history of rights for children

In 1919, a remarkable woman named Eglantyne Jebb wanted to help children who were dying of hunger as a result of World War I. She founded an organization in the United Kingdom called the Save the Children Fund. Four years later, she wrote a special set of statements: a list of children's rights. Jebb said that her goal was "to claim certain rights for children and labor for their universal recognition." This meant that she wanted worldwide agreement on children's rights.

It was many years before countries around the world agreed that children have rights, but eventually the statements became recognized in international law in 1989. They are now known as the United Nations Convention on the Rights of the Child (UNCRC). The rights in the UNCRC are based on the idea that everyone deserves fair treatment.

Almost every country has signed the UNCRC, so it affects most of the world's children. The rights it lists cover all areas of children's lives, such as the right to have a home and the right to be educated.

The students of Luricasha School in Peru elect a student council to discuss their rights and responsibilities.

Elementary school students in Colombia talk about how to make their rights into realities.

Rights for all? The UNCRC should mean that the rights of children everywhere are guaranteed. However, this is not the case. Every day, millions of children are denied their rights. Children may suffer discrimination because they are poor or disabled, or because they work for a living. It might be because of their religion, race, or whether they are boys or girls.

Children are very vulnerable, so they need special care and protection. The UNCRC exists to try to make sure that they are protected.

The right to a good home Many of the articles in the UNCRC are about every child's right to a good home. With a good home, children have a place where they belong, are loved and cared for, and can grow up safely. Here are some of the articles:

Article 9 You have the right to live with your parents unless this is bad for you.

Article 20 You have the right to special care and protection if you can't live with your own parents.

Article 27 You have the right to a good enough standard of living for you to grow and develop properly.

This book tells the stories of children around the world who are achieving their rights.

Children who are poor have the right to a good home

A safe place Homes can be made of brick, stone, wood, cloth, or straw. They come in many different shapes and sizes and keep us warm and dry. But a home is more than just a building. Home is a place where we belong, where there are people who love us and look after us. All children need a good home if they are to live safely.

The right to a good home Many children come from poor families, and their home may not be much to look at. But all children, whether rich or poor, have the right to live at home with their parents unless there is a risk to their well-being at home—for example, if their parents are addicted to drugs.

"One day my mother explained that there was no money to rent the house."
Benjamin, 14, Democratic Republic of Congo

Homes come in all shapes and sizes. They may be built of bricks, like these in England...

...or made of canvas, like this tent-like "ger" in Mongolia.

Homelessness   Sometimes a family has to move out of its home because the parents do not have enough money to pay the rent. Homes can be destroyed suddenly by a disaster, such as a flood or an earthquake. Sometimes war or violence forces families to move to a safer place. What do you think it would feel like to have to leave your home in a hurry?

Life can be hard   Once you have lost your home, everything else becomes much more difficult. It can be hard to concentrate on schoolwork, even if there is a school to go to. You have nowhere to keep your belongings, and may even have nowhere to cook your food or find shelter from the rain and cold.

Staying healthy is also a problem. It is difficult to keep yourself and your clothes clean. When you are homeless, it is easy to get sick but hard to see a doctor or buy the medicine you need. You may even become separated from your parents. Homeless children may face all of these problems and more. The UNCRC says that no matter what happens to children, they should be looked after properly by adults.

Projects in many countries help homeless children find a place to live where there is someone to look after them.

These homes in Mali are made of mud with a thatched roof.

9

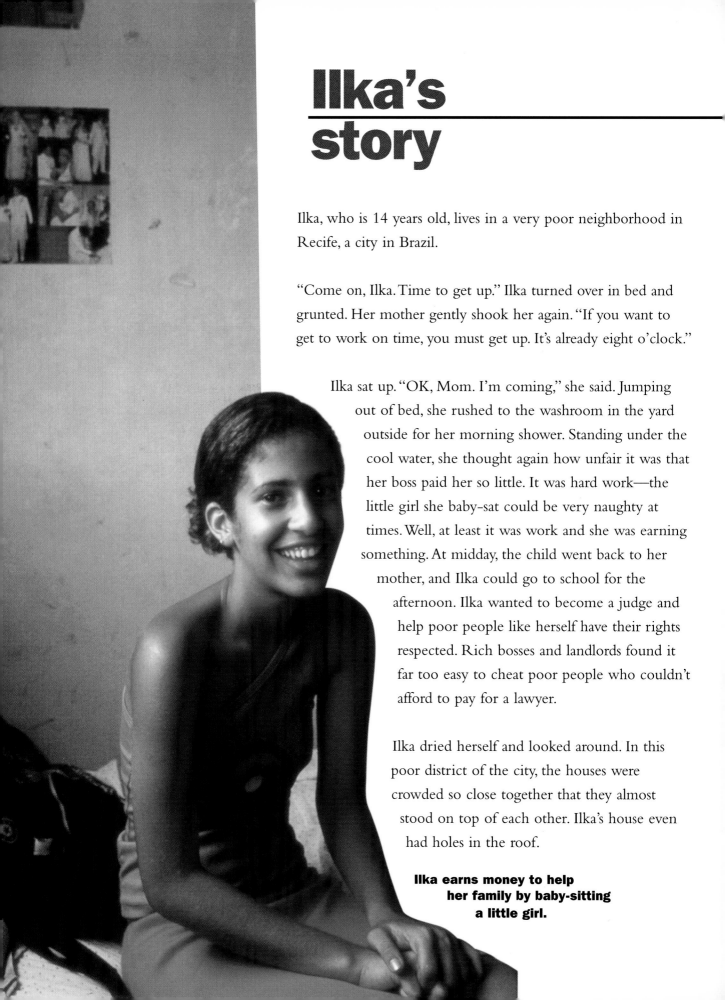

Ilka's story

Ilka, who is 14 years old, lives in a very poor neighborhood in Recife, a city in Brazil.

"Come on, Ilka. Time to get up." Ilka turned over in bed and grunted. Her mother gently shook her again. "If you want to get to work on time, you must get up. It's already eight o'clock."

Ilka sat up. "OK, Mom. I'm coming," she said. Jumping out of bed, she rushed to the washroom in the yard outside for her morning shower. Standing under the cool water, she thought again how unfair it was that her boss paid her so little. It was hard work—the little girl she baby-sat could be very naughty at times. Well, at least it was work and she was earning something. At midday, the child went back to her mother, and Ilka could go to school for the afternoon. Ilka wanted to become a judge and help poor people like herself have their rights respected. Rich bosses and landlords found it far too easy to cheat poor people who couldn't afford to pay for a lawyer.

Ilka dried herself and looked around. In this poor district of the city, the houses were crowded so close together that they almost stood on top of each other. Ilka's house even had holes in the roof.

Ilka earns money to help her family by baby-sitting a little girl.

The rain leaked in, and mold was growing on some of the walls. They did not have the money to get the roof fixed. Ilka's father had remarried and had a second family to look after. She often saw them at his market stall, but he never came to visit his first family. And he gave them very little money these days.

Ilka and her friend Fabiana often talk about their dreams of a better life.

Ilka smelled coffee. Her mom was in the kitchen making breakfast. Some of Ilka's friends had to make their own breakfast, if they got one at all. Others didn't live at home any longer and slept in a tiny room where they worked. "I'm lucky to have such a good mom," Ilka thought, "and although our house is not much, it's where I belong." Ilka pulled on her clothes and went to join her mother. She threw her arms around her. "Thanks for everything, Mom," she said.

Ilka attends gatherings that help her and her friends catch up on the schooling they miss when they have to work.

Children in danger have the right to a good home

Although this Colombian family has lost its home, the family has managed to stay together.

When there is war

Whenever there is conflict, there is the danger that ordinary people will be hurt and their houses damaged. They may have to leave home to find a safer place to live until the fighting is over. Sometimes they can stay with relatives or friends in another part of the country. If they have nowhere else to go, they may have to stay in a camp or hostel. Sometimes they even have to leave their own country and go to another to find somewhere to live.

Tonight, 20 million children won't be sleeping in their own beds because they have had to leave their homes due to war. This is more than a third of all the children in America. Some of these children have had to move several times. Many have become separated from their families and are trying to survive alone.

Living in a camp

When children live in a temporary camp, it is often hard to find food to eat or clean water to drink. If they left home in a hurry, they may have only the clothes they were wearing at the time. They may have to live in a tent, which is cold in the winter and hot in the summer.

An unnatural life When children have to leave home because of war, it means they can no longer do normal things—such as go to school, make friends, or live in a proper house. They have to leave their toys behind, and there is no television to watch. Life can be very boring.

Separated families Sometimes children become separated from their parents and have to search for them. While they are looking for their families or waiting for the war to end, it is important that children have somewhere safe to live and that someone is watching over them.

Tracing families During the war in Kosovo, from 1998 to 1999, "family tracing posts" were set up. These places helped family members try to find each other using mobile phones.

DID YOU KNOW?

Seven million children are refugees in countries other than their own. A person is made a refugee somewhere in the world every 21 seconds.

Thirteen million children are "displaced." This means they are homeless within their own war-torn countries. A displaced child can be away from home for many years.

When there is war, many people have to live in camps, like this one in Kosovo, until it is safe to return home.

13

Saranda's story

Saranda in the room that her father had to rebuild. The house was badly damaged in the war in Kosovo.

Saranda lives in western Kosovo. When she was 12, heavy fighting between Serb forces and the Kosovo Liberation Army took place all around the area where she lives, and her family had to move several times to find somewhere safe to live. This is Saranda's story:

"When we ran from home the first time, the police came to our door and said we needed to leave immediately. We left with just the clothes we had on. After about a month, we thought it was safe to go home.

"The second time, we saw Serbian soldiers shelling the next village. We were afraid, so we went to our aunt's place in another village. After a week, the Serb forces came and said that we had to leave that village. So we ran again and went to another village nearby. Afterwards, they sent us to Albania, where some people gave us a room.

"I felt very bad about leaving my home. You can't explain the feeling when you are thrown out of your house by force. I was afraid that I would never return, and that I would never see my father again. I just wanted to cry and cry and never stop.

Many Kosovans had to stay in camps like this one when it became too dangerous to stay in their own homes.

"When we were coming home, I felt very good because finally I was returning to my home. When I got there, I saw that it had been shelled. The door was open, the roof had collapsed, and the rubble was up to my knees. We couldn't even walk inside. In the beginning, we didn't have a tent or anything like that, so we lived under a cardboard shelter that we made ourselves. We ate and slept there for two or three months after we returned from Albania.

"I don't think it's right for us children to suffer like this. I hope that all Kosovar children can live in peace and freedom, continue our interrupted lessons, and become somebody so that we can help our country and all the countries of the world."

Saranda's father, who is a construction worker, was given the help he needed to repair their house. The family is now able to live inside it in safety once again.

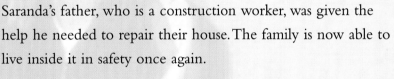

Refugees are given help to find family members who have become separated by war.

Children without their parents have the right to a good home

When parents aren't there

Sometimes children cannot live with their parents because their parents are sick or have died or have had to leave because of war. It is always important for children to be cared for properly so that they can grow up healthy and take part in the life of their local community and the wider world.

DID YOU KNOW?

By 2010, there will be 44 million children under 15 who have lost one or both parents to AIDS.

When special care is needed

Some children need special care because they are sick or disabled. Some families have enough money to provide the extra care, but others don't, so some children have to leave home to be looked after. The children may need to take special medicine, or may need equipment to help them, such as ramps and wheelchairs. Some children are so sick that they need to have someone with them all the time to make sure they don't hurt themselves. When parents are not able to provide this extra care, the children may have to live in a boarding school or home that can give them the equipment or care they need.

Some children leave home to find work. These children work all day making carpets by hand.

Leaving home Sometimes children make their own decision to leave home. Their mom may have remarried, and they may not get along with their new dad. Sometimes they run away because they are unhappy at home. Children who leave home like this can easily find themselves in trouble unless they find somewhere else to live and be looked after. They are too young to be able to look after themselves.

This young girl in Cambodia is breaking rocks to earn money for her family. The stones will be used to build roads.

The need to work Some families are too poor to be able to look after their children properly. In developing countries, the government usually is not able to help either. So the older children may leave home to earn money to help the rest of the family. Most countries have laws to try to stop this from happening, but it is hard when families need to find ways to earn money so that they don't go hungry. Many families try to keep all their children at home, even if some of them still have to work.

17

Sarah's story

Sarah is 10 years old. She lives in a village near Arua, in northwestern Uganda. Four years ago, her father died of an AIDS-related illness, leaving behind Sarah, her nine brothers and sisters, and their mother. Sarah says:

"I don't remember much about my father, but he was a carpenter. When he died, my heart broke because I was told suddenly that he had died."

Since her father's death, life for Sarah and her family has been a struggle. Sarah explains:

"Since then we've really suffered, because we don't have enough food. We sleep on papyrus mats, and we don't have blankets to cover ourselves. We use old clothes instead."

Sarah at home in Uganda. "This house isn't very comfortable," she says. "I'd like to have a permanent house made out of baked bricks, with an iron sheet roof."

Sarah works hard from the moment she wakes up at 6:00 A.M. She sweeps the house, then she lights the charcoal-burning stove to heat water so the family can wash and have tea. At 6:30, Sarah leaves the house to walk to school. The journey takes her an hour. Sarah likes school and is eager to learn—one of her goals is to become a member of parliament (MP). But it costs money to go to school in Uganda, and if Sarah isn't able to pay the fees, she is sent home. When this happens, Sarah says, "I feel miserable because I'm really interested in education and in learning, so when I'm stopped from learning I feel bad."

Children's charities are helping Sarah continue to learn by supporting her local Sunday group. Attendance is free, so Sarah doesn't have to worry about school fees. At the group, Sarah has learned about AIDS and how to prevent it. Sarah says she prefers her Sunday group to her weekday school because the classes are more fun.

"We also have nice songs to sing and it's more imaginative," she says. "We also do drama and play volleyball."

Trained volunteers also visit families like Sarah's who have lost one or both parents to AIDS. The volunteers give the families advice about children's rights and how to avoid AIDS. They also help with practical things such as arranging house repairs. Sarah is determined to help others in the future.

"I'd like to be a nurse to help HIV- and AIDS-affected people. I want to be an MP, too. If I become an MP, I'll help my mother. I'll also help my younger sisters and brothers to go to school. And I can help other children by teaching them about dangerous diseases like HIV and AIDS."

Sarah enjoys the Sunday classes. She says: "I also like working with other children, because you can make friends and share things together."

Sarah plays volleyball with her friends at the Sunday group. "In the future," she says, "I'd like to have clothes, shoes, and to be in school."

Children who live on the streets have the right to a good home

Life on the streets Some children leave home thinking that life on the streets will be better, because their parents are too poor to look after them. Many such children plan to look after themselves by finding jobs and earning their own money. But they soon find that it is not easy. There may be people who rob them or beat them up. It is not easy to find work, and it is hard to find somewhere safe to sleep at night.

Getting into trouble Sometimes children leave their homes because they are unhappy. Often they have nowhere else to go and end up living on the streets. Then they miss school and fall in with a bad crowd or become hungry or sick. They might begin to take drugs to try to forget that they are alone. They may start to steal or become involved in more serious crime and then find that they are in trouble with the police. Once this happens, it becomes even harder to return to a normal life.

Street children in the Democratic Republic of Congo collect garbage for recycling.

Help for street children

Children's charities work with government officials and volunteer groups, helping them set up welfare services for street children. These groups often have staff members who walk the streets to meet homeless children. They tell them about the help they could receive in the care centers. The centers provide food and schooling or skills training so that the children will be able to find proper jobs. Sometimes they are able to give the children somewhere to sleep. If it is possible, they try to find the child's family and encourage them to live together again.

Living on the streets can be dangerous. These boys in Cambodia are putting their health at risk by sniffing glue to keep themselves from feeling hungry.

> "Life on the streets is very risky, and you're always desperate for money."
>
> **Thao, Vietnam**

Benjamin's story

Benjamin lives in Kinshasa, the capital city of the Democratic Republic of Congo.

When Benjamin was little, he lived with his mom, dad, and three brothers and sisters. His dad was a soldier, and his mom sold onions to earn a little extra for the family. They had lots of fun together. But one day there was a new president in the country, and Benjamin's dad was sent to work in another town. At first, everything was fine. The family spoke to him often by radio, as there was no phone connection outside the capital city. His dad always sent them money. But he got sick and came back home, too sick to work. Then he died. That was when life really changed. Benjamin says:

"One day my mother talked to us and explained that there was no money to rent the house. She said that we would have to go and live with her parents. Then Mom told us that she had to go away on business, so we could have some money. Since then she hasn't come back."

Benjamin sells water as part of a project that was set up to help street children earn money.

Benjamin's grandparents found it hard to look after the lively young family. They couldn't afford to buy the food the children needed. Then Benjamin's older brother ran away. At first no one knew where he was or how to find him. Then, one day, Benjamin saw him walking along the road.

"He told me that it was better to live on the streets, so I left home, too. There are many jobs you can do. You can help people to park their cars. Or you can call taxis for customers."

But Benjamin has found that life on the streets is not always good. He is often hungry and afraid.

"Sometimes I sleep at a place for street boys run by a priest, and sometimes I sleep on the street. Living on the street can be dangerous. Like now, there's a killer going around. We're afraid of that."

Benjamin knows that living on the streets is not a good life. He misses home and having a family to look after him.

"I can say that the way I am now is at least a little better than before. But I don't want to stay like this all my life. It has to change," he says.

Thirteen-year-old Jimmy also sells water to thirsty people in the market.

Children who have to work have the right to a good home

"If I had a magic wand, I would change everything about my life." Ana, Guatemala

Some children have to work Children whose families are poor often have to work to help earn enough money to buy food and clothes and pay the rent. Many families try to stay together so that they can help each other. Sometimes, however, the children have to leave home because the family cannot afford to look after them. It is not necessarily a bad thing for children to work, but they need to work in safe places and have enough time to go to school and to play.

Children who are sold or loaned Some families are so poor that they "sell" one of their children to work so that the rest of the family can afford to buy the food they need. Sometimes the buyer promises that the child will earn lots of money to send home to help—but this is often a lie. Some children never see their families again because the buyer sells them to someone else. If the children cannot write and have no money, they find it impossible to contact their families. Others are "loaned" by their parents to factory owners, who hire the child to work for six months or a year.

Hussein's help on the family farm in Ethiopia means they can all have a better life.

These girls in Kashmir earn money by selling the cloth they have carefully embroidered.

In Vietnam, Anh dropped out of school to catch and sell shrimp to earn money for food for his family.

Families who stay together Even though the children of many poor families have to work, most of them live at home. Often they help in the family business. They may help to run a small café or make crafts to sell. Sometimes they walk around the local street during the day selling food or cleaning shoes. When night comes, they go home and share their earnings with the family.

The problem of poverty Ideally, no child should have to work, but families who are struggling to survive do not have any choice. The main task for those trying to help working children is to tackle the causes of poverty, but it takes time to change systems and governments. So, in the meantime, projects are set up to find realistic ways to help children who have to work. They focus on improving children's lives by protecting them from dangerous work and providing them with schooling so they can find a good job when they are older.

Ana's story

Ana's home is a village in the mountains of Guatemala. Her mom works in a bakery, but since her husband died, it hasn't been easy to earn enough to look after eight children.

When Ana was 10, she agreed to leave home and go to the city to look after her cousin's child, but now she looks after four-year-old twins for someone else. The family lives in a large house, and her boss treats her well, letting her share a bedroom with the family. Ana is now 14 and sends half of what she earns to her mother.

The twins go to school every morning, so Ana gets up very early to make packed lunches for them. While they are out, she washes and irons the clothes so that she can play with them in the afternoons after school. She's also learning how to cook.

"When the twins get back at noon, I play with them all afternoon—I look after them and give them everything they ask for. I love taking care of the children."

Ana is really excited because she goes to special weekend classes for girls who have to work during the day. The project has helped Ana learn to read and write. She does her homework after the children have gone to bed.

"At first my boss wasn't sure if she'd let me go—she said I had to clean the house first. It's important for me because if you can't read or write, it's difficult to find a job."

Ana enjoys living with a family in a big house and eating good food so that she can grow strong and healthy. She is also very happy that she is able to earn money at the same time to help her mom give her brothers and sisters a good home. But she still misses her own family very much.

"In my spare time, I do my homework—usually while the twins are asleep."

At this project in Guatemala, household workers like Ana learn about their rights.

"My mom came to visit me at the beginning of the year. I was so happy to see her and that she could spend the day with me. If I had a magic wand, I would change everything about my life. I would like to live with my family in my village."

Learning to read and write has made a big difference in Ana's life. Now she would like to continue studying and hopes to become a teacher.

27

Glossary

AIDS Acquired Immune Deficiency Syndrome; AIDS is caused by a virus that attacks the body's immune system and makes it unable to fight off disease

article A part of a legal document, such as a convention

children's rights The rights that everyone under the age of 18 should have, including the right to life, the right to food, clothes, and a place to live, the right to education and health, and the right to be protected from danger

conflict A serious disagreement between two or more groups of people that can lead to fighting

discrimination The unfair treatment of people because of their race, religion, or whether they are boys or girls

displaced people People who have had to leave their home because of war or a natural disaster but stay within the same country

exploitation Unfairly taking advantage of a person; for example, if an employer pays children very little for working long hours in a factory

export Something that is made in one country and sold to another

founded Started

hazardous Dangerous

HIV Human Immunodeficiency Virus; the virus that leads to AIDS

less developed countries Countries that have few industries and in which many people are very poor

poverty A lack of money that results in a poor standard of living

projects Plans set up to improve life for local people

refugees People who leave their home country because they feel unsafe

street children Children who are homeless and live on the streets of a city rather than with their family

temporary camp A camp where people who have had to leave their homes can live until it is safe for them to return

United Nations An organization made up of many different countries; it was set up in 1945 to promote international peace and cooperation

Index

Additional information

Books

Bennett, Paul. *War: The World Reacts*. North Mankato, Minn.: Smart Apple Media, 1999.

Castle, Caroline. *For Every Child: The UN Convention on the Rights of the Child*. New York: Dorling Kindersley Publishing, 2001.

Lobe, Tamara Awad. *A Right World: Helping Kids Understand the Convention on the Rights of the Child*. Washington, D.C.: Youth Advocate Program International, 1999.

Web sites

www.childrensrights.org/
The Children's Rights organization site

www.rcmp-grc.gc.ca/youth/childrights_c.htm
A site that explains the Rights of the Child in child-friendly language

www.savethechildren.org/
The Save the Children organization site